Pulling Out All the Stops

Pulling Out All the Stops

A Simple, Straightforward Guide to Drive Your Business, Career & Life Forward

Kelli Rogers

BeyondVisionary
Personal & Professional Coaching
Dallas, TX

Pulling Out All the Stops

A Simple, Straightforward Guide to Drive Your Business, Career & Life Forward

Copyright © 2015

Beyond Visionary Personal & Professional Coaching
www.beyondvisionary.net

Cover Art: Nicollette Mollet / NicolletteMollet.com
Hair Stylist: Johari Ransom
Makeup Artist: Keyanah Jones

Disclaimer: The purpose of this book is to educate and inspire. This publication is sold with the understanding that the author is not engaged in rendering psychological, professional or legal services. If expert assistance or counseling is needed, the services of a competent professional should be sought. The author and publisher shall have neither liability nor responsibility for any loss or damaged caused, directly or indirectly, by the information contained in this book. Your success is predicated upon your work ethic, delivering extraordinary value, and serving others with excellence.

Printed in the United States of America

I dedicate this book to my ladybug, Virginia Ann Earley-Johnson.

Made on purpose, with a purpose, for a purpose!

When You Can't Imagine Life Without Her

When they said, "Time heals all wounds," I'm sure,
they didn't consider my mother's love so pure.

Because when I'm no longer led by her words so wise,
or cautioned about life through her discerning eyes.

When she can no longer give me a hug so tight,
or pray over me daily with words just right;

When it's no longer her "Hello" over the phone I hear,
it is then that those unhealed wounds re-appear.

But when God said, "Joy comes in the morning," I'm sure,
He did consider my mother's love so pure.

You see, because it was Him who granted her wisdom,
I know it's through Him my help still does come.

Because it was Him who taught her to hold me,
His hands – should I allow – will continue to mold me.

Because through God's grace her undying spirit can guide me,
my wounds are mended with peace knowing mother is inside me.

-T' Eileen Liggins

Thanks Auntie Terri! The echoes of these words are endless… Love you!

Table of Contents

Stop letting NO knock you down

Stop listening to negative thoughts and limiting beliefs

Stop being cheap and start investing in yourself

Stop convincing yourself you don't have time

Stop thinking you can do it all by yourself

Stop trying to be all things to all people

Stop reinventing the wheel

Stop talking about it and start doing it

Acknowledgements

First and foremost, I want to thank my Heavenly Father for creating me to be a visionary, and using me and my gifts to impact the lives of others. Dear God, now allow the words in this book to provide clarity and encourage those about to quit, put stumbling people on their feet, and fresh hope in those about to collapse. In Jesus name, Amen.

This book would not have been possible without the support and encouragement of my husband, Lacorey Rogers. Thank you for understanding my long nights and early mornings at the computer and your patience with me for taking on yet another project, in spite of the time it took me away from you.

Thanks to my dad, George Johnson, my brothers/bodyguards, Kyle Earley, Kamron Johnson and Chandler Johnson, and my mother in-law, Brenda Hall, for always believing in me. Your admiration and constant feedback has been my inspiration and motivation for continuing to improve my knowledge and advance my career forward.

I owe a huge thanks to Nicollette Mollet, for the time and effort you spent illustrating my book cover. The work you do speaks for itself and I'm confident that your skills and creativity will result in a boost in sales for this book. You did an excellent job!

I'd also like to thank my hair stylist, Johari Ransom, and makeup artist, Keyanah Jones, both the best in the business. Your intimate touch and commitment makes me not only *look like* but also *feel like* the prettiest girl in the world.

Words cannot express my gratitude to Leneisia Fletcher and Danuel Jackson-Smith, for their candid advice and assistance in polishing this manuscript. And I want to personally thank all the thought leaders, mentors and coaches who have educated, inspired and influenced me in writing this book.

Last but definitely not least, those who have supported me throughout my career, thanks for EVERYTHING. I really appreciate each and every one of you!

Preface

Pulling Out All the Stops is a simple, straightforward guide to drive your business, career and life forward. Often times, we pity ourselves because we are not where we want to be or think we should be in life, not realizing that we are the cause of our own circumstances. Whether it's through the decisions we make, the actions we take – or fail to take – or the people we surround ourselves with, we attract who and what we are. Once we let go of the fears, limiting beliefs and people that hold us back, it's then that the skies become the limit. Success is for everyone, not a select few. And we alone have the power within ourselves to solve our problems, relieve our anxieties and pain, and improve our circumstances.

We are habitually coached to take the next step, go for it, keep moving forward, and try new things. But sometimes you just have to STOP in order to move forward. Sometimes you have to stop doing the wrong things in order to start doing the right things. With focus on self-awareness and performance, Pulling Out All the Stops presents eight behaviors that you must stop, in order to start living the life you've always imagined.

Kelli Rogers hopes to motivate readers to faster results by building their confidence and transforming their attitude, as she provides a different perspective on common issues and daily challenges that we face individually and professionally. "I've overcome challenges, experienced life-changing events, and mastered skills that don't come easy to others. In the process, I've discovered my purpose, which is to utilize my knowledge, experiences, and skills to guide people towards their goals and watch them fulfill their dreams." This book allows readers to practice strategies discussed and make improvement in their lives, without having to ask others for help.

Introduction: A Universal Stop

Stop signs are almost fully universalized throughout the world. If presented with a red octagon with white writing, I would be willing to bet my last dollar that you would stop immediately. But, have you ever wondered why a stop sign has eight sides?

In general, the greater number of sides on a sign, the more dangerous the upcoming stretch of road is. A circle (which is considered to have infinite sides) designates the riskiest hazards, like railroad crossings. An octagon denotes the second most dangerous conditions, like intersections. Within this context, the eight sides of a stop sign epitomizes eights dangerous behaviors that stop us from achieving our goals.

Your life should be about "finding the intersection of the world's greatest need and your greatest passion." However, there's a reason it's frequently necessary to stop before entering or crossing any intersection. Failing to do so is one of the most common causes of accidents. In order to achieve better results in your business, career and personal life, it is equally important to STOP, get to know yourself and become more aware of what you need to do differently.

CHAPTER 1

Stop letting NO knock you down!

"When you go in search of honey, you must expect to be stung by bees."
–Joseph Joubert

I was born into entrepreneurship, as both of my parents had their own businesses growing up. My first few jobs were in retail and customer service; therefore, I eventually evolved into a great salesperson. I honestly believed that I had not only developed excellent sales techniques but I even mastered the psychology of sales. So once I finally convinced myself to start my own professional coaching business, I was confident I would have no problem getting clients. So many times I've heard, "you can sell anybody anything," I never thought twice about being rejected or what if they say "NO."

Along with my retail, customer service and administrative skills, I also carry a creative side. Since I was in the startup phase, I decided that it would be more cost-effective for me to create my own business cards and marketing materials. However, I did not do this depending upon my own talents and expertise. I researched advertising and content creation and sought feedback regarding the attractiveness and effectiveness of my materials and products. I worked with my business coach to develop marketing strategies that would magnetize my target audience, and I listened to almost every marketing guru and coach that I came across for additional tips and advice.

After practicing my marketing message and sales pitch over and over again, I was determined to hit the ground running. I visited several small businesses to discuss the challenges they were currently facing in achieving their business goals and how my coaching products and services could help them experience better business results. My plan was to leave each business with a scheduled consultation or contact information for follow up, and on day one I was proud to schedule a consultation for the following week with a Body Wrap consultant. "Mission accomplished," I said to myself as I spent the rest of the week preparing for our next meeting, confident that I left a good impression and my potential client eager to find out more.

Tuesday morning at ten o'clock is when her consultation was scheduled and I was right on time, which unfortunately for me is very rare – *I'm just being honest.* I was ready with my pen and notebook in hand, accompanied by a few questions to gather more information about the current state of her business and her dreams for her future. However, before I could even offer my coaching services she adamantly advised she was not interested in my coaching program at this time and she will continue trying the things she currently had in place. To make a long story short, she told me "NO!"

No two words have the power to change our lives more than YES and NO. In fact, one of the first words children learn to recite is the word NO. Until recently I was like most people, I did not like or react well with rejection. Growing up, when I needed to seek permission or had a specific request, before asking I would brainstorm and strategically analyze every possible outcome. The first question that I had to answer was how bad did I want it? Did I want it as bad as I want to breathe or did I just kind of want it? How important was it that I have, do or go wherever I was asking? What was the benefit of me doing, having or going where I wanted? The next thing I considered was realistically, how likely am I to have this request granted? Would I be more likely to receive what I wanted if someone more credible presented the proposition on my behalf? For example, mommy can you ask daddy if I can go to the Valentine's Day dance with David this Friday..? Or can you have your mom call my mom and ask if I can sleepover this weekend..? Or can you ask my parents if I can go to Six Flags with you all..?

Sometimes the mere thought of hearing NO paralyzes us and keeps us from asking for the things we want or need. And it's usually because of limiting beliefs or resentment from past experiences that we develop this fear of rejection. We get so shy, too nervous or scared to make our needs or request known and, as a result, we experience difficulty in taking action. We worry ourselves with "what if they say NO," and ultimately end up going without. We would much rather wait for someone to approach us with hand-outs and we forget to consider, "what if" no one ever offered us anything? What if everyone around you were getting the things they want in life while you are left with whatever is available, sometimes nothing? Don't let NO dictate or determine your destiny. Ask for what you want and learn to deal with rejection effectively. "A closed mouth doesn't get fed," which means if you don't ask the answer is always NO. Instead of wondering and wrecking your brain with "what if they say NO," figure out how you can make them say YES. Colonel Sanders, founder of KFC, had his idea and recipe rejected 1009 times over a period of two years before a restaurant finally accepted it. The moral of his story is you have to need what you want so bad that NO is not an option.

We have all been rejected, which I know doesn't make the feeling suck any less. When we are told NO we feel inadequate, defeated, undeserving and unsupported. As a result, we become discouraged, even frustrated, and we begin questioning our purpose and abilities. Hearing NO not only slows us down, it often stops our progress and causes us to change activities. But guess what?? Life is about going for things and when you do, rejection is always a possibility. Accept that things will not always work out the way you want them to and that's okay. For instance, just because you ask someone to marry you and they say NO doesn't mean you give up on love and marriage. You would move on from them but you wouldn't quit asking people out, right? Let go of past rejections and denials, and never give up! Failure and rejection is only the first step to succeeding, so think of every loss as a lesson and every win as a blessing. Seek feedback and be inspired to work harder for your dreams and desires. When you make the decision that your dreams and goals are nonnegotiable, you won't take NO for an answer.

Stop letting NO knock you down. Don't give that two letter word the power to phase you. Roll with the punches and keep fighting for what you want. If they say NO, just say NEXT. Man's rejection can be God's redirection. God sometimes uses rejection to move us to a new place or assignment, where we otherwise would not be. You may have thought your idea was a good opportunity but God has something much better, and what God has for you is for you. Adopt a favor-minded mentality and know that

He will not only supply all your needs, He will also give you the desires of your heart. NO should never translate as a closed-door but Next Opportunity. Turn rejection into redirection and quickly move on. Remember Dr. Seuss? Of course you do. Nearly every child has read "The Cat and the Hat" or "Green Eggs and Ham." Yet, Theodore Seuss Giesel had his first book rejected by 27 different publishers. Think about it, what if Dr. Seuss would have given up after the first five or ten NOs? In the same manner, remember the book Chicken Soup for the Soul? Authors, Jack Canfield and Mark Victor Hensen, were rejected by over 140 publishers before eventually becoming bestselling authors. Their book sold over 100 million copies, and the Chicken Soup series was launched.

People tend to believe NO means NO, but rejection doesn't always mean defeat. Being rejected simply means that the relationship or situation is not working, ideal, a priority or the best fit, at least for the moment. Failure and rejection, however painful, can lead you to identifying where you went wrong, providing a chance to reconfigure and find the best path to continue – yes, I said continue! Seek to gain insight and perhaps refine your approach. You learn from the past to create a more successful and satisfying future, so reframe the rejection and be positive. NO actually means I don't want exactly that, I can't commit to those terms, or I can't figure out a way to make that happen. Therefore, NO is your first opportunity to problem solve and signals the beginning, not the end, of a value-creating negotiation. Again, NO should never translate as a closed-door but Next Opportunity. Learn to believe in yourself and not be swayed by the naysayers. Without rejection or failure you'll never fully experience your true greatness. Steven Spielberg was rejected by University of Southern California School of Theater, Film, and Television three times before becoming one of the greatest movie directors of all time as well as most influential film personality in the history of film.

So the next time you make a request, make the specifics as clear as possible and remain confident in your intended results. Focus on facts and highlight the benefits and values. Push for what you want and never be afraid to ask, *"why not?"* You will be rejected and you will hear NO. Change your attitude, it's not always personal. NO affords an opportunity to make the concessions necessary to make everyone happy. Ask questions like, what stands in the way of you saying YES? Is there anything else I can put on the table that would give you the value you need to close this deal? Is there any additional information you need from me that would help you sell this proposal to your company/board/organization? Think of NO as a simple conversation starter and recognize that behind every NO is a YES waiting to come out. Therefore, shift your focus on making people believe in you and your cause, and present an offer that is intriguing and irresistible. And do not expect to get without giving. Seek to serve and develop a trusting relationship. Create a sense of urgency and consistently follow up. This allows them to take you more seriously and causes them to reconsider. Make it easy for them to say YES. Truth is, "the world is full of genies waiting to grant your wishes." (-Percy Ross)

CHAPTER 2

Stop listening to negative thoughts and limiting beliefs!

"You are what you believe yourself to be."
–Paulo Coelho

How many times have you heard yourself say, "I'm just not good with money... I'll never get the job I want... No one will ever want to marry me... I always seem to screw things up... I'm not smart enough... Things need to be like or look like this before I can start..." or any sort of negative message? Many of us have negative thoughts and messages, like these, that stand in the way of our success and limit the choices we make in life. Those are limiting beliefs.

As is the case with all beliefs, whether positive or negative, a limiting belief starts off as a single thought in your mind in reaction to a certain event, or to what you were told by your parents or society in general. This thought is repeated often enough until it is accepted as a reality by your subconscious mind, which stores all your previous life experiences, your beliefs, your memories, your skills, all situations you've been through and all images you've ever seen. I, myself as an entrepreneur, have had to overcome and continue to conquer many negative thoughts and limiting beliefs in order to grow my business. I remember constantly thinking my marketing content isn't good enough, because I wasn't receiving the response I was expecting from my target audience. As a result, I was unable to attract clients.

But did you know you can attract absolutely anything you desire in life using the power of your subconscious mind? Really! The Law of Attraction states that whatever you give consistent thought to, you will create. Once you have given great thought to something with great emotion and then expect it to come, it will. Your thoughts are powerful magnets and you will get what you constantly think about, whether you want it or not.

Unfortunately, the majority of people don't know they have limiting beliefs because they seem so real. These people go along day after day doing and saying the same things over and over, all the while wondering why they never reach their goals. They don't realize that it's our beliefs that shape our life and sometimes keep us from achieving the quality of life we are seeking. So if you are not where you want to be in your life, whether physically, emotionally, romantically, financially or professionally, the chances are that an underlying, deeply ingrained, negative belief is limiting your progress and causing your unwanted circumstances. Let's use something we all can relate to as an example, MONEY. Now it may appear that it is because you are struggling with your finances that you believe you are bad with money, but the true causality runs in reverse. It is your limiting beliefs about money that's creating and perpetuating your unwanted financial circumstances. Since you likely see others living the life you want and achieving the things you desire, you know that your goals are possible. You simply have to listen to what you're telling yourself and recognize the situations you continually find yourself in. When you rid yourself of limiting beliefs, anything you want in life becomes possible.

Limiting beliefs are often fear-driven and are caused by faulty logic or poor estimation of probabilities. They almost always begin with "I can't... because..." such as, I can't find a decent paying job because I never completed college. As soon as you say the word "because" you invoke a part of your brain that believes "I have a reason." And that's when you simply stop trying. So as long as you tell yourself that you can't do something because... you never will! All breakthrough starts with a change in your beliefs.

A key way by which we form our beliefs is through our experiences, particularly when we are young. We act, something happens and we draw conclusions. But when we allow our history to restrict us, or let self-doubt and low self-esteem control us, what we are actually doing is giving power to the people around us who also doubt and don't support you. The real truth is we are not limited by anything other than our own personal thoughts and beliefs. No one's life is pre-determined by history, their childhood, family or society because the events of our lives don't control our lives, our decisions do. And we allow our negative thinking to limit our success.

Stop listening to negative thoughts and limiting beliefs as well as people who don't support your visions and goals. The surest way to transform your mind and your life is by identifying and changing the beliefs that aren't helping you live the healthy, happy, enriched life you want to live. Realize we live in a time when what is possible for each person is determined by what that person believes. You have everything you need to take your business, life or career to levels you've never imagined, and it starts with your mindset. When you change your perceptions and open your mind to new possibilities for your situation, what seemed like a hopeless circumstance can instantly transform into endless opportunity. Change your beliefs so that they matchup to the beliefs of those who have what you desire. Surround yourself with people living their dreams and make sure your values are aligned with theirs.

Overcoming your limiting beliefs is essential for personal and professional growth. One technique for overcoming limiting beliefs that works for me is positive affirmations, which are simply positive statements specifically targeted at re-programming an existing negative belief. Remember, a belief is a thought that you keep thinking. Therefore, if the new, positive statements are repeated enough times, they will in time be strong enough to over-ride your existing negative thoughts and beliefs.

Another method for overcoming your limiting beliefs and building self-esteem is to act "as if." This is similar to positive affirmations; however, rather than using your thoughts and words, you are using your actions. It means to act *as if* you do not have your negative beliefs or, even better, *as if* you have what your mind is telling you don't. You may have heard it said like this - "fake it, until you make it." For instance, if you lack confidence, notice how it feels to walk around with your head held up high and your shoulders back. When you do this often enough, your mind will "forget" your lack of confidence because your new bodily stance sends a very strong, over-riding message of confidence.

Creative visualization is one of my favorite methods for re-programming your subconscious mind when overcoming limiting beliefs. It's essentially the process whereby in a relaxed state of mind and with your eyes closed, you focus on what you want to accomplish while believing that you already have that which you want in the present moment. Creative visualization imprints the picture of your desires on your subconscious mind in order to actually bring them into your life. It involves you using all of your senses... *What do you see? What do you hear? What do you feel? What does it smell like?* Visualize how you would think, talk, act and feel if you were living the life you've always imagined and had those things that you desire. Once you bridge the gap between your beliefs and imagination, you are able to attract whatever it is that you want without fail.

The final technique, and your first priority, for overcoming limiting beliefs, is "know thyself". And part of knowing yourself is to understand your beliefs, your deepest desires and emotions, your character traits, your values, what makes you happy, and why you think and do the things you think and do. How can you realistically set goals, go about life and have successful relationships if you don't know who you are or what you want? You really can't. To know thyself is to be aware of your strengths, weakness, likes and dislikes. Knowing yourself is being observant and aware of your moods, reactions, and responses to others and what is going on around you. Not knowing yourself will lead to confusion and cause you to create or succumb to negative thoughts and limiting beliefs. However, self-knowledge helps you figure out what you want to work on and what you are willing to let go. Really getting to know and understand yourself better moves you to a place of self-acceptance and increased self-worth, and in turn leads to better decision making, setting and reaching appropriate goals and ultimately living a more productive life.

In a nutshell, developing an overall positive mind set and monitoring your self-talk are fundamental to overcoming limiting beliefs and creating the life you dream for yourself. So stop telling yourself what you can't do and start convincing yourself that you can do whatever you put your mind to. What you believe, what you fear, what you expect, all directly affect what you do. If you've already made up in your mind you can't do something, then it's over; the handwriting is on the wall and the fat lady has sung. Refuse to entertain any doubt or negative thinking about your dreams and believe that you can have, and God wants you to have, whatever you desire to have.

CHAPTER 3

Stop being cheap and start investing in yourself!

"You have brains in your head. You have feet in your shoes. You can steer yourself any direction you choose. You're on your own. And you know what you know. And YOU are the one who'll decide where to go."
–Dr. Seuss

When I first started my business I would often get discouraged. It seemed like every time I spoke to someone about my coaching products and services, their response was either "I don't have the money right now" or "I can't afford it." I felt as though I had to give discounts, slash my prices and give my first born child just to make a sale. Later, I saw these same people's activity on social media or heard through the grapevine that they "got a new car" or "spent the whole day shopping" and sometimes even called it "retail therapy," or "good times with good friends." This made me realize that these people aren't flat broke. It's not that they don't have the money or means of getting their hands on any; they just don't see the value in what I am offering. "I can't afford it" really means I do have the money, but if I purchased this I have to give up some of my conveniences or make a few lifestyle changes and I'm not willing to do that, or it's more important for me to hold onto my money right now. So by discounting and slashing my prices for those who claim they "can't afford it," I wasn't really doing them a favor or helping them get ahead in life. I was actually devaluing myself. And as a result, I was often stuck in situations where it was hard for me to profit, essentially telling those people you're right, my services are worthless.

Even the poorest people *find* money to acquire the things they value or can't live without. Some people value a well-balanced meal. Some people value celebrating birthdays and holidays. Some people value a luxurious lifestyle, with a TV the size of a bus. Trust me; one thing I know for sure is when we really value something it's not hard to get our hands on the cash to get it. Why? Because people afford what they believe to have value. If I told you, you have been invited to an event next weekend with some old classmates I bet you will find money to get an outfit, new pumps, hair done, nails done, the whole nine. We rarely differentiate between cost and value, especially when it comes to those things we really want. We will happily spend money eating out, at happy hour, going to the movies or whatever. However, when it comes to paying for knowledge, content, and other valuable resources or things that should be considered an investment, we hesitate. We come up with 99 other ways to spend our money or try to acquire those things for free. In fact, we've gotten so used to getting things free that when these things start costing money our reaction is a salty "no way!" Now let's be real, who doesn't love freebies? But have you ever noticed that when we get things for free we don't value those things as much. Things that come easy and free are often taken for granted. Using our hard-earned money to pay for our belongings and possessions gives us a sense of accomplishment, pride and ownership, causing us to value those goods or services more. We take things we pay for a little more serious and will take the actions necessary to get what we want out of our life or business.

Many people operate with the "only if it's free... or cheap" philosophy. The problem with this is many times we sabotage ourselves by being cheap. Not frugal but cheap. Let's start by clarifying the difference between the two. Cheap people concern themselves with the cost of things, or the amount of money that is required to complete their purchase. Frugal people, on the other hand, care about value or the usefulness of a good or service. Cheap people shop for the lowest price on everything, while frugal people try to get the lowest price on most things but expect to spend more money on items that are of value to them or a higher quality. Being frugal means displaying some responsibility and good judgment in the way you spend your money as opposed to showing off or trying to impress people by making unnecessary purchases. Now I'm not saying don't look for bargains or take advantage of handouts, saving money is smart. Even multimillionaires want to save money. But I have to admit my biggest mistakes were caused by me trying to save a buck or two and settling for the cheap stuff. In the end, my attempt to save money cost me more in the long run, which means in some cases we are saving money by choosing to pay more. A lot of people nickel and dime the really important things that could pay off explosively. I witnessed this in Barnes & Noble's a couple weeks ago, as I overheard this lady telling a young girl about a book she was trying to encourage her to buy. The young girl, in her super cute designer frames responded, I can't afford to buy this book today, it cost $27.95. The woman further explained to the young girl that the book was such a good read that it previously inspired her to do something that made her $10,000 in less than a month. Now I'm not sure if the young girl was this lady's daughter, extended family, friend or just another customer in the bookstore but she continued trying to convince this girl to spend her money on things that will benefit her both financially and intellectually. She ended the conversation by saying, "don't let your cheapness hold you back because it definitely won't help you get ahead." How powerful, right?

Stop being cheap and start investing in yourself. Investing in yourself is all about becoming a better you – your skills, knowledge level, health and any other part of your life that will improve your ability to earn more money, make better decisions and live a more fulfilling life. Warren Buffett once said investing in yourself is the best thing you can do. "Anything that improves your own talents; nobody can tax it or take it away from you. They can run up huge deficits and the dollar can be worth far less. You can have all kind of things happen. But if you've got talent yourself, and you've maximized your talent, you've got a tremendous asset that can return tenfold." To summarize Mr. Buffett, you are an asset. Think about that for minute. If you work for someone else, you are an asset to that company. If you're married, you are an asset to your spouse. If you have children, you are an incredible asset to them. You're an asset to the community you live in, to your neighbors and to those you interact with on a daily basis. Most of the time, when I hear people talk about being an asset it has to do with their possessions, accomplishments and skills in the workplace, which is certainly important if you're trying to keep your job, advance your career or enter a new line of work. However, it's equally important on a personal level. These two aspects of your life are more interconnected than you may imagine. Investing in your professional life will impact aspects of your personal life, and investing in yourself on a personal level will undoubtedly help you on a professional level.

Too many workers make the mistake of working their butt off for their employer and not making time to invest in themselves. Of course, working hard for your employer isn't a mistake in itself; it's smart for a lot of obvious reasons. But what's not smart is spending so much time and effort growing your employer's business or platform that you don't spend time on your own dreams. Don't work so hard for someone else that you forget to invest in yourself because if you don't invest in yourself no one else will. And like Mr. Buffett said, your talent is the multiplier. The more energy and attention you invest in it, the greater the yield. Identify your talents, skills and abilities and find ways to turn them into a solid, income-generating career.

I once spoke to a group of women about investing in themselves and in their dreams. As I prepared to share with these women, I came across a quote by Benjamin Franklin which read "for the best return on your money, pour your purse into your head... Pour your purse into your mind and your mind will pour back into your purse." We came to the conclusion that this quote means instead of investing or setting money aside for the interior home makeover you've been so excited about or taking that vacation you've been eagerly planning for months, invest not only your money but also your time and energy in things you want to accomplish.

Some people are scared or choose not to invest because they don't want to lose money. Everyone wants a high yield investment but not everyone believes it takes money to make money. Truth is, you have to be willing to lose something in order to win or gain anything. The promise of high returns also comes with high risks. Investing in yourself is by far the most profitable, low-risk investment you'll ever make. It yields not only future returns often a current payoff as well. Investing usually increases in value, while most of the "stuff" we buy decreases in value over time. Don't be crazy and think that I'm implying that people should deprive themselves of material possessions, that's just ridiculous. But I am suggesting cutting back on unnecessary spending and making investments now that will help you build a solid, financial future. Some of the most successful people earned a relatively modest income but also lived below their means, enabling them to invest for a better quality of life.

The surest way to achieve a better quality life, to be successful, productive and satisfied is to place a priority on investing in both personal and professional growth. Develop your skills and advance your education by taking classes to obtain degrees and relevant certifications. An investment in knowledge pays the best return. Take advantage of available training resources such as workshops and seminars, attend conferences and participate in webinars. Expand your knowledge by reading books and literature related to the talent or skill you want to work on. Keep current and stay abreast of the latest trends and cutting-edge advancements by subscribing to publications, reading blogs by experts and following the latest news feed.

Invest in yourself by exploring your creative side. Choose an activity you've never tried, haven't practiced in years or never fully explored. Discover the outside world through traveling, gardening, landscape, photography, and art. Creativity in any form helps us grow personally and professionally, and there is a fountain of creativity in most of us that has never been tapped or certainly hasn't been used to its highest potential. Invest in yourself by nurturing your mind, which allows you to have more to give now and in the future... more energy, more knowledge, more compassion, more ideas, greater strength and physical and mental endurance. Learn a new language or how to play a musical instrument, try gourmet cooking, or write a book, short story or poem. Experience culture by listening to different styles of music, attend performances or join an organization or group comprised of people from various backgrounds. Engage in courageous conversations and keep your mind active by playing word games or board games that include strategy. Nurturing your mind by learning new things and keeping your mind active even in simple ways helps to grow and maintain your mental ability.

Care for your body and invest in your health. Your body is like a well-oiled machine. If you care for it in the way you might maintain an expensive car, it will perform marvelously and last for a very long time. Make healthier food choices as often as possible and remember, you truly are what you eat. What you eat plays a large role in your energy and ability to perform. Exercise and go to the doctor regularly, and use protective maintenance such as vitamins. Believe it or not, rest and relaxation is just as important. Slow down and don't overload your system. Be sure to take care of the outside too. Get a fabulous haircut or hairstyle and wear clothes that make you feel comfortable and attractive. I know you've heard the infamous Deion Sanders quote, "If you look good, you feel good. If you feel good, you play good. If you play good, they pay good. If they pay good, you live good."

Investing in yourself truly makes a difference in your life, your well-being and your ability to thrive and perform to the best of your ability. The extent to which you invest in yourself, mind, and body not only shapes the way you interact with the outside world, it often reflects the opinion you have of yourself.

If you don't take anything else from this chapter please understand that there's really no better investment you can make than in yourself. Investing in yourself not only enhances your life, your career, your money and your happiness, it will improve the lives of those around you. You can't just live life passively and expect great things to come your way. Your future, which is where you are going to spend the rest of your life, is in large part determined by your willingness and ability to invest in yourself now. Your money won't grow if you don't grow, and your life will only get better when you do, so do something today that your future will thank you for.

CHAPTER 4

Stop convincing yourself you don't have time!

"It has been my observation that most people get ahead during the time that others waste."
–Henry Ford

It's 6:30AM, the start of a new day but not much different from the day before. So much to do but only 17½ hours left to get things done, if I haven't pressed snooze one too many times. The first half-hour consists of my daily devotional time to thank God for waking me up and giving me the strength to crawl out of my warm, cozy bed. I speak words of faith over my day and praise Him in advance for the divine favor that is sent before me and the blessings that are about to rain all over me today. After I have conditioned my mind for the day, I spend the next fifteen to twenty minutes conditioning my body and maintaining my fitness with a quick, workout routine. Then off to shower and get all dolled up in my quest to take over the world (yelling to Pinky in my Brain voice). The rest of my day is usually consumed with about 10 hours of emails, phone calls, meetings, presentations, marketing, networking, coaching clients and, hopefully, new consultations, before rushing home to feed and cater to my hubby as well as a little playtime with my super-spoiled dog. As I prepare to call it a night, I review my to-do list and beat myself up about all the important things I was unable to complete today, that are now urgent tomorrow, all because "I didn't have time."

Last week a colleague of mine reached out to me to see how I was doing and if I need additional help with a project I was working on. My response to him was not unless you can give me a few more hours in a day. I was joking but serious at the same time. On several occasions I've thought to myself, if I could have anything in the world, it would be more time. I'm sure we all encounter many of days where we feel we have so many things to do but not enough time to get them done. With the need to do more and more in less and less time, more hours in a day is something that everyone wants yet it's impossible to achieve. Time is a precious commodity. We only get a certain amount of it and then it's gone forever. Basically, you use it or lose it. We might not be able to create more time but at least we can eventually figure out how to manage our time effectively, to do all the things we want to do.

Now you can argue that nobody has time to do everything because our options are endless but our time is limited. Truth is it's not about "having" time; it's about "making" time. Everyone gets the same 24 hours a day, seven days a week and at the end of the day we make time for what we want. Too many of us claim we can't achieve success because we lack the time to pursue the things that are necessary; however, isn't it funny how we make time to scroll through our social media feeds or watch a television series each week and refuse to let anything interfere with it? Although time is what we want most, it's what we use worst. We may not have time to do everything we could do but there's definitely time to do the things we *should* do if we seize the moment and manage our time effectively.

When we feel like we don't have time for something that's almost always because either we have *not chosen* to make time for it, or we have *chosen not* to make time for it. Yes, there are plenty of times when I would love to do something but it just doesn't work out because it's not worth it for me to make time. Maybe it conflicts with something else I have already committed to doing, maybe it cost too much money or maybe I'm just too tired to do one more thing. Whatever the reason I still have the ability to choose whether or not I want to make time for it. To say I don't have time is like saying *I don't want to* or *it's just not a priority*. Every day we make hundreds of decisions as to what we will and will not make time for.

Pay close attention and be more protective about how you spend your time, and recognize when it's being wasted because businesses aren't built wasting time. How many hours have you spent at a restaurant for lunch or coffee to acquire information that could have been given over the phone or sent in an email? Believe it or not, time is more valuable than money. If we waste money we can always make more of it, but if we waste time we can never get it back. Make sure you are using your most precious resource in ways that are more rewarding to you. Make time for the things that matter the most, things that will grow you and make you more productive. Build habits and routines around things that are going to add value to your character and help you become better than you were the day before. Spend more time trying to make something of yourself and less time trying to impress others.

As much as we instinctively cling to those things that make us feel busy, there's no such thing as being too busy. Don't be fooled, busyness is a form of procrastination, and procrastination has been called the thief of time, opportunity's assassin and the grave in which dreams are buried. If you really want something you'll make time for it, if not you'll make an excuse. And while you're making excuses someone else is executing. Somewhere in the world there's a single mother who comes home after a day's work to put her children to bed and then, despite being exhausted, spends two hours writing a chapter of her book that she wants to get published. Somewhere in the world there's a married couple who grinds all day, tends to the kids and then stays up until 2AM writing a proposal for their catering business that they are trying to expand. Somewhere in the world there's a full-time student with a full-time time job that awakes after only getting two hours of sleep to complete a research paper and study for final exams. The bad news is yes, time does fly, but the good news is you are the pilot so you control how you spend your time. Spend more time executing and less time making excuses. Spend more time producing and less time procrastinating. Figure out what it is that you really want and make it a priority. If its success, than you have to do what other people are not doing to get it. And guess what? Successful people are stingy with their time.

Stop convincing yourself you don't have time. Many people never live their dreams because they use time as an excuse to procrastinate and avoid getting things done. Don't put off till tomorrow those things you can get done today. The best time to do something is usually right away. Avoid laziness, idleness, disruptions and other things that rob you of the time you need to achieve your goals. There are so many things competing for your attention and most of those things can potentially waste a lot of time. If you haven't already noticed, technology can really sabotage our time, leading to procrastination and hindering our productivity. Studies have shown it can take anywhere from five to fifteen minutes after an interruption or distraction has occurred for a person to gain back the momentum they had before the disruption. By minimizing our distractions and interruptions like internet, social media, television, cell phones, radio, etc., we make time to accomplish things that are worthwhile and will help us become even more successful. Narrow your focus on what matters most and avoid committing yourself to things that eat up your time. Sometimes we simply do not have enough time because we spend too much time on unnecessary and low value obligations that tie us down and keep us busy, yet at the end of the day we feel like we haven't accomplished anything. We get caught up putting out fires or wasting time on activities that we have little to no control over or simply take up too much time. It's okay to say no to things that are of little importance or can be done later.

Too often how we spend our time is on a thought in terms of *"what am I going to do today?"* or *"what do I do next?"* Effective time management, however, is a carefully developed strategy to determine how to use our time. Create a scheduling ritual with an accurate, detailed plan of how you will spend every bit of your time each day. Identify your priorities and set clearly defined goals that are realistic and achievable. Use a calendar for daily priorities and a project chart for long-term commitments. Complete the most important or most difficult tasks first because immediate action generates momentum for further action. To boost our productivity many of us like to multitask, or do multiple things at once. But contrary to popular belief, multitasking doesn't make us as productive as we think. In fact, multitasking could be costing us time instead of creating it. Several studies have found that multitasking can actually result in us wasting about twenty to forty percent of our time. Why? We can't really focus on more than one task at once. When we switch tasks our minds must reorient to cope with the new information, while dealing with feeling overwhelmed and stressed. Eliminate, delegate or automate unimportant task and learn shortcuts to simplify activities, using systems, tools and processes that will save you time. Unfortunately there will be times when something urgent comes up and cannot be avoided so plan for the unexpected by setting aside time in your day to deal with these urgent issues without sacrificing your priorities.

Time is free, but it's priceless. You can't own it, but you can use it. You can't keep it, but you can spend it. Once you've lost it, you can never get it back. And what's even scarier is, if you don't master your time, it is of a much higher probability that you will become an unconscious slave to people who have mastered theirs.

CHAPTER 5

Stop thinking you can do it all by yourself!

"Alone we can do so little; together we can do so much."
–Helen Keller

Have you ever seen a young child try to dress himself? For my two year old nephew, the buttons are most difficult. He concentrates on each as though it's the world's most important problem and only he can solve it. And while his determination to do it himself is admirable, the result is often a late start for the day and a shirt with undone buttons.

Independence is probably one of the first long-term goals that we set or consider for ourselves. *I want my own car... I want my own apartment* or *my own house... I want to own my own business...* We have all had that mindset of *I don't want to depend on anybody for anything...* Some of us get so caught up in our independence that, even when necessary, we hesitate to ask for additional support or assistance.

Why do we strive to be so independent today? Maybe you feel like asking for help or support is a sign of weakness or inferiority, after all we are supposed to be the expert. Heck, that's why we run businesses, right?! How would it look if we were to ask for help? Here's the simple truth: we hate to ask for help because we think it makes us look weak; because we're proud and we perceive the ones offering help as being judgmental or doubting our abilities; because along the way our parents and teachers rewarded us for accomplishing amazing things all by ourselves (ahhh); because somehow we got mixed up in a work culture that implies that asking for help is cheating. I, myself, have struggled with asking for help because I feared needing help was a sign that I lacked professionalism or was incompetence. Still today, I occasionally have difficulty allowing others to help me because I am a perfectionist with creative visualizations and I prefer to be in control of my own choices, results and consequences.

But we all depend on one another for all kinds of things, don't we? Society was just setup this way. You can't produce everything you need yourself. We as people have to rely on other people in some way for our survival. Different functions are allotted to different people for the welfare of everyone, so that we will coexist better and live more effectively. Instead of independence it is much healthier to live interdependently. God designed us for connection with him and to build relationships with each other. When we are interdependent we are prepared to ask people for help and to help people when they need us. We open ourselves up to others and allow others to open themselves up to us. We walk through life together rather than on our own. We build bridges to each other's islands. We learn from each other, we encourage each other, we support each other, we care for each other, we have fun together, we make memories together and we help each other grow. We realize we are stronger and better as two or more then we are on our own.

I don't care how smart you are, how organized or efficient you become, or how good you are at your job; you can only do so much on your own. What I have managed to learn over the years is that asking for help takes humility. Assistance is often there if we have the courage to ask for it. I love how life will put us in situations where we have no choice but to go to others for support, comfort or relief. And those who choose not to reach out get held back and become stuck in their circumstances, forfeiting their chances of progress, triumph and success. By refusing to accept help, we ignore the fact that we are social beings who need to cooperate with one another to ensure that we thrive. Too often we fail to realize or take for granted that every single person that we come in contact with has something that we don't; something unique and special to offer to offer us. Don't miss out on the opportunity to learn new things and work with so many different people who show up in your life and have something to offer you because you're hell-bent on trying to do it all yourself.

When you are trying to live a full, productive and effective life, it's easy to fall into the trap of trying to do it all yourself. Whether this means micromanaging at work or dealing with every little thing at home, it can initially seem like a way to make sure things are done properly. Before long, of course, you end up feeling frazzled. You find yourself spending a lot of time doing things that aren't as important and shouldn't have taken as much time as it did, you're overworked, and you don't ever seem to get the chance to pursue activities that really excite you.

So, why do we spend such huge amounts of time trying to do things we need not be doing ourselves and probably suck at anyway? Things that people around us can and will do for us, if we are willing and able to hand them off. Possibly it's money worries that make you think you have to do all your own work. Possibly you're worried about control and think, "no one will do it quite as well as I do it" or "I don't feel like explaining this, so I'll just keep it on my plate." It may seem that doing things yourself has many advantages: you can save money; you have everything under control, etc. But it also has some serious downsides, and overtime, they clearly come to outweigh the advantages for us. So if you're someone who's Mantra is "if you want a job done well do-it-yourself," there are two crucial ways to reduce this burden: you need to eliminate and delegate. Maybe you need to hire someone to clean your house, let your spouse or older kids take a turn cooking, pay an accountant to do your taxes, or outsource very simple and routine work-related tasks. Whether it's a personal or work obligation, look for ways to delegate. You can only do so much by yourself.

In the early development stages of my coaching business, I insisted on doing it all myself. Not because I wanted to, mind you, but because I just didn't have the right support team in place to delegate. Fact is, we're pulled in many directions so a key element to getting things done is learning how to delegate effectively. Once I formed a team and learned the secrets of delegation, I started not only achieving better results but I also found myself having tons more time and peace of mind. I was able to use the work provided by others and mold it into my own style of delivery and go off and do the things I really wanted to do, things I am good at, things that are important to my business.

Stop thinking you can do it all by yourself. Many entrepreneurs view themselves as superheroes, trying to do everything themselves because it sounds glamorous. But NEWS FLASH: No one gets to the top by working solo. Success is a team sport. Even a marathon runner must thank their trainer, coach and nutritionists. Speak to some of the most successful people in any industry and they all mention their "team." Mentors, advisors, associates, secretaries and family members all contribute to the success of the one person. Yes, a lot of your success is a combination of factors such as background, hard work and attitude, but it mostly comes down to your relationships.

There's no limit to what you can accomplish if you don't care who gets the credit. Trusting another team member with completing or contributing to a project not only gives you time to regroup, but also allows them to showcase their ability. When done properly, delegation improves efficiency by allowing you to transfer work to people whose skill sets better match the task. Delegating routine work will relieve some of your daily stressors and allow more time for you to tackle other things. Finding out what each team member enjoys doing most and assigning associated duties increases the chance that they will put more thought and effort into completing the assignment because they actually enjoy it. As a leader, delegating jobs to appropriate, qualified staff is one of the most important skills you can develop and is crucial to business advancement. If you are unable to trust your team with your vision, advancing to the next stage of the project, tier of clients or level of business is stunted.

No one learns, grows or achieves anything in a vacuum. If you've been successful, I know for a fact that you didn't get there on your own. Somebody along the line gave you some help. There was a great teacher somewhere in your life. Somebody helped to create this unbelievable American system that we have that allowed you to thrive. Somebody invested in roads and bridges. If you have a business, you didn't build that. Somebody else made that happen. All of us have had someone nurturing us and helping us to grow and develop. We know that we didn't get where we are on our own, and that we have an ongoing responsibility and dependence on others for our continuing enjoyment of the goods of human existence.

It takes a village to get things done and run a successful business. Most successful entrepreneurs don't just plan for the products and services within the business; they also strategically assemble a team of resources or their "village" to help support the company. And as an entrepreneur, you have more support and resources available to you than you realize. From mentors to workshops to networking events, there are plenty of brains to pick out there. Connect with those who can help you. The more you learn, the more you grow. And the best way to gain confidence is to engage with and learn from the experiences of others in your community who are already doing what you want to do, and doing it well. Your business will move forward more quickly when you tap into and leverage the power of interdependence. There is a special kind of magic that is created when a community of support and profound wisdom is formed.

So stop with the *I got this... I'm good...* and *I don't need anybody...* Don't let your pride shut out those extending their services to you because you feel vulnerable and would rather be self-sufficient. Take the load off yourself and save some time and energy by delegating tasks in your personal and work life to other people. Having support and assistance from others actually enables you to feel more secure and enhances your personal development. You are the master of your craft, so who is it that you need to surround yourself with that has the "other" skills to make your business a success and your dream a reality? As social beings, interdependence with those around us is essential to ensuring our survival. Allow others to serve you. It is a lot more satisfying having someone to scratch your back for you, than trying to do it yourself! Network your way to success...

CHAPTER 6

Stop trying to be all things to all people!

"If you want to live a happy life, tie it to a goal. Not to people or things."
–Albert Einstein

As my husband and I strolled downtown LA looking for a spot to grab some lunch, we passed a sign that read *Smoothies – Chinese – Sushi*. We both looked at each other strange, as the one of us asked "so this place really serves up great smoothies, Chinese and sushi?" We both then agreed that we did not want to find out. I mean, would you actually trust a smoothie joint for really good sushi? Does the combination even sound appetizing?

Throughout my experiences I've learned that there are three secrets to failure; two include trying to please everyone and trying to do everything. Many aspiring and season entrepreneurs and small-business owners operate with a *we-do-it-all* mentality, and sales pitch, wanting to offer an array of products and services and give their customers many options. Unfortunately, their good intentions produce opposite results. On one hand, when you give your customers too many options they become confused and are less likely to buy. On the other hand, if you allow yourself to be pulled in a number of different directions, you will lose focus of the vision and goals on which your business was initially built and inhibit your ability to grow your business to its full potential. We are all familiar with the expression, and may even believe in the sentiment "jack of all trades, master of none." Well let me tell you how Wikipedia defines the expression: jack of all trades, master of none "is a figure of speech used in reference to a person that is competent in many skills, but is not necessarily outstanding in any particular one." By spreading yourself over so many areas you will never be able to fully develop in one area.

If you could be known for just one thing, what would it be? Instead of trying to do it all, figure out what it is you do best and concentrate your efforts in those areas. Forget what you're good and perfect what you're great at. As a business owner your purpose is to hone and deliver your core competency - the one thing you do better than anyone else and customers are willing to pay for - as quickly and efficiently as possible. Recognize the value of what you have to offer and then align yourself with those people who can most benefit because there is no way you can sell to everyone. It's okay to experiment with a little bit of everything but find an area you enjoy the most and focus your attention on that. And once you find your niche do everything you can to be the best that it. Don't ever stop learning about it. Continue perfecting your craft and become the leader in your space. People who become wealthy by monetizing their skills are wealthy only because they are the very best at what they do.

When you can do it all, you can never be the best at one thing. Finding or creating a niche is the key to success for even the biggest companies. A niche is an area of interest or expertise – it's your specialty. In certain industries there is a lot of competition between companies that sell similar products or services; therefore, in such a crowded marketplace, a niche serves the critical function of distinguishing you from your competitors. Rather than trying to serve every customer and getting lost in the crowd, use your skills and expertise to cater to those who have unique needs. Become a specific thing to specific people. For example, open a maternity clothing boutique that specializes in corporate/professional wear, or a law firm specializing in immigration cases. Become clear about your expertise, talents and abilities and how to leverage them in your business. When you stop trying to be all things to all people you do your best, most impactful and most satisfying work. Focusing on a niche can be an effective and profitable strategy for small businesses because it is often too difficult and costly to try to cater to very broad audiences.

Additionally, when you are trying to be everything to everyone, your message becomes vague and is less impactful. Instead of trying to appeal to everyone, a small business often does better by developing a specialty in an area that is not being fully served by other businesses and exploiting that need with cost-effective marketing strategies. Think of a niche as a hook that will help you reel in potential customers that you have identified as the most profitable and likely prospects for your business. Niches are by definition narrow, but not so narrow that they don't contain enough customers to sustain the business. The secret to defining a profitable niche is to find an area where there is an unmet demand and to fill that need with your products or services.

Stop trying to be all things to all people. It's not even realistic to expect to meet the needs of everyone, no business can. And honestly, trying to appeal to every type of customer undermines trust and turns people off. Successful companies know who their customers are and who their customers are not. Who is it that needs what you are selling? It's so easy to fall into thinking that everyone should want your product, your service, your customer experience but, unfortunately, it just isn't so. There are people out here – nice, normal, good people – who don't need what you are selling. Small business success is dependent upon identifying a substantial pre-qualified group of customers who are willing to purchase your products and services at a profitable price point. As an entrepreneur, you must reach those specific customers and understand as precisely as possible what they want to satisfy their particular needs. Get to know them very well. Determine what your customer values and then strive to exceed their expectations. Creating a customer profile and well-defined target market will help you tailor your message and business offerings to differentiate your business and uncover the benefits of your products and services.

Business owners often make the mistake of defining their customer base too broadly, making it very difficult to engage in effective marketing efforts. Remember, if you are marketing to everyone you will attract no one. By choosing a specific market you can develop products better suited for that market than competitors, making it easier to sell. And contrary to popular belief, defining a target market will not limit your business. You can still expand your practice or services from "one-to-one" to "one-to-many." New entrepreneurs sometimes resist choosing a niche or defining a target customer base, thinking it might reduce the number of potential customers, but actually the opposite is true. When you are clear about what you are best at and learn to share it with the world, business finds you. Identifying target customers does not prevent your business from accepting customers that don't fit the target profile. If such a customer seeks your product or service, you will still be available. By simply focusing on what you do best, success will follow.

So how can we gather the necessary information about our customers' wants if we are marketing to everyone? It's impossible. You'll have a much easier time competing against the big dogs if you're focused on serving a specific need very, very well. Most small companies can't compete against big corporations when it comes to reaching an entire market, so if you can carve out a slice of that market - define it and serve it well - you can own it. Pay attention to what your competitors are doing and then position your business to serve your target market in terms of the essential things that your competitors are not providing. Try to determine one or two critical factors that lead to the customers' decision to choose one business over another. It may have to do with products, some aspects of your service, your pricing or possibly the friendliness of your employees. What's important is to understand what customers want, and not to push on them what you think they should want.

The process of finding and studying potential customers for your venture doesn't have to be complex or expensive, but it is extremely important. In a nutshell, defining your target customers means identifying specific characteristics of people or businesses who you believe are most likely to buy your product or service. It requires you to find out everything you can about the customers whom you intend to pursue. Once you have that information, you'll have a much better chance of capturing those customers for your business. Common characteristics used to classify customers include: age, gender, income level, buying habits, occupation or industry, marital status, family status, geographic location, ethnic group, political affiliation, hobbies and interests and their needs.

The key to success in business is not coming up with a genius idea. It's not about having a better product, although that doesn't hurt. It's not about having the lowest price. The key to success in business does not even lie in creating a unique, cool and otherwise awesome experience for the customer. The key to success in business is finding and filling a niche or gap, if you will, filled with people or organizations with key needs or wants that are going unfulfilled. You have to have something that distinguishes you from what's already available. What unique qualities and benefits set you apart from your competitors? And remember, no matter how great your product, service or customer experience, no one product, service or business is perfect for everyone.

"How do I get more customers?" is a problem that most entrepreneurs and businesses face every day. Bottom line is you can't be all things to all people. People hire specialist to help them solve problems not generalist. Narrow your focus and marketing and be as clear and specific as you can, deciding exactly who you want to attract and serve as customers, so you're able to serve them much better. Without a focus, you'll never be able to make the difference that you potentially could. Take your niche market and grow it, not the other way around, by using your expertise to build your business. Remember the goal is to use your specialness to focus your business, corner your market and then make them seek you out. And above all, avoid being that jack of all trades and master something!

CHAPTER 7

Stop reinventing the wheel!

"Some of us learn from other people's mistakes, and the rest of us have to be the other people."
–Zig Ziglar

O nce upon a time, I had a mentor that gave me some of the best advice I've ever received. He said, "If you want to be wealthy, hang out with wealthy people and study what wealthy people do. If you want to be funny, hang out with funny people and study what funny people do. If you want to be poor, hang out with poor people and study what poor people do. If you want successful, surround yourself with others who are already successful and study everything those people are doing." Why? Well just in case you haven't caught on by now, we naturally mimic the behaviors of those around us.

Last month I was coaching a new entrepreneur and she said something that really made me think. What she said was a reflection of the type of mindset I find common in many new and seasoned entrepreneurs alike, including myself. In fact, what she said was something I have struggled with and still think about and face on a regular basis. If you're a high achiever, an entrepreneur, or business owner you may face this problem too. *So what is that problem?* The problem is we falsely believe that we must reinvent the wheel if we're going to be successful or start something new.

When I first started Beyond Visionary Personal & Professional Coaching, I knew I wasn't the only person showing individuals and businesses how to achieve better results in their life, career, or business. Actually, I knew of at least a hand full of other coaches pursuing my same target audience. However, I wanted to inspire and be a catalyst for change as well. I wanted to use my own voice, share my own experiences, and put my own motivational messages out into the world. But enough about me, let's get back to the comment this young entrepreneur made during our most recent coaching session. As we were reviewing the business model of someone she admired in her industry, she said, *"Well, I could just copy what he's doing."* When she said that, I immediately stopped our conversation to point out the brilliance of what she had just said.

It's easy to get caught up in the idea that only select people are lucky enough to become successful. It seems as though they are the "lottery winners," so to speak, whom we often hear about and aspire to be like but find it nearly impossible to replicate their success. As a woman who went from being overworked and underpaid in the social work field to a full-time entrepreneur, I can tell you that becoming successful has little to do with luck, and a lot to do with finding what works for you and sticking with it. If you want to be a big success in any area, find out what other successful people in that area are doing, and do the same things, until you get the same results.

I often wonder why many entrepreneurs never seek guidance from peers, mentors, or experts. Instead, they try to figure everything out themselves, many times reinventing the wheel, meaning a great deal of time or effort is wasted creating something that already exists. And unfortunately, they are not alone. Right now, other ambitious business owners and leaders are too suffering. They are trapped in conference rooms and boardrooms debating over how to solve a problem. The kicker is that the problem has already been solved, just not by someone in the room, and solutions from outside are ignored. But why do that to yourself? You don't have to solve every problem you face on your own. Somewhere, someone has already solved your problem, or at least substantial portions of it.

When you find an obstacle in your way, whether it's trying to figure out *what* to do or *how* to do it, you usually have a few options. You can try to learn everything you can about the topic or problem you are facing to figure out why we are stuck, find a workaround that will let you move forward without solving the problem, or give up and try a different approach. Now I know some of you are thinking all these options are unattractive because each take a lot of time and none of them are guaranteed to work. Sometimes those really are your choices but very often someone has already faced this problem, solved it and published the solution. Listen to that voice in your head that says, "Wait, there has to be a way to do this." Know when a problem is probably already solved and how to successfully find the solution to that problem before you invent your own.

One of the most important skills you can possess is knowing how to learn. No matter who you are or what you do, there are always things you don't know and things you could benefit from learning. Successful people believe that learning never ends. This doesn't mean they're going to school to get a new degree, although they may. Even without formal education, they're constantly reading and learning from others around them, perhaps from books, articles and magazines, conferences and seminars, or from others who are already where they want to be. As Brian Tracy says, "Success leaves tracks." It's these tracks, which are the behaviors and habits of those doing great things, that set them apart from the ordinary folks who just work their nine to five jobs and never look to get ahead. So if you looking to do great things in your business, career or personal life, you need to be able to look up to somebody who has done something similar, or who exhibits the qualities you are striving for, even if only to prove to yourself it can be done. Be a sponge and absorb other people's experiences, finding out what works and what doesn't. There's no harm and a lot to gain from looking at what everyone else is doing. Pick and choose what you want to emulate, you don't have to accept everything. Be a student of other people's folly and mistakes and use them to help you become better. The more you learn about the brick walls others charged into head first, the more likely you are to avoid them.

A primal motive for reinventing the wheel is that people don't know what's already been done. Ignorance, one way or another, is the leading cause of wasted effort everywhere. And the obvious cure for that ignorance is knowledge. People who don't spend the time studying the problems they are trying to solve are bound to reinvent something and likely not nearly as well. There are only so many ways to design a website, marketing campaign or even a product strategy. Instead of driving your team into further brainstorming sessions, it would be wise to ask: Who else has tried to solve this problem? And can we learn from what they have done?

The second reason for reinvention pertains to ego and reward. In many industries and organizations, there is more prestige to be gained for making something new than reusing work done elsewhere in the company or industry. This is true even when the newly made thing is much worse than what already existed. The verbs "make," "invent" and "create" leads to more promotions then "reuse," "borrow" or "convert." We sleep on the fact that everything old can be made new again. And sometimes it's not just that we need a new solution, we need a better solution. The solution that already exists is simply not good enough. Never mind the fact that this solution works wonderfully for every other human being, we think we have a better way. What works for everyone else won't work for us because we have special circumstances. We convince ourselves that we're different.

Some say that patent laws drive many to reinvent, but this is simply a cop-out. Anyone who has read a few patents knows that they are limited to very specific kinds of ideas. A wise competitor can study, learn and apply those lessons without resorting to theft or copying. There's a time to reinvent and a time to reuse, and the best minds know that both approaches have their place. Take a process that's already proven to work for many people and make it your own with small tweaks and changes.

Stop reinventing the wheel. Too often we think we have to reinvent the wheel in order to be successful. We believe we have to do something completely different in order to call it our own and achieve what we want to achieve. But if that were the case, Wendy's would not have opened nearly thirty years after the very first McDonald's. If that were true, Walmart would have never opened its doors after Target had already been in business for sixty years. While it's important for entrepreneurs and business owners to define their own processes and test innovative ideas, many waste time, which is your most valuable asset, or miss key insights by not learning from others. Sometimes we just need to copy the methods of someone who has already gone before us and been successful doing something we want to do as well. This is not to say that someone else's solution will always work for you. Of course, what works for Company A may not work for Company B. Every problem is different in some way, and no solution fits all. Different people and companies have different goals, different abilities and even different definitions of success. Identify what is unique about your problem and isolate those portions. Define these unique portions so that they are as small as possible. Then it will be worth your while to make the rest of your problem fit one or more previous solutions so that you can concentrate on your small, unique portion. Your solutions to your unique portions will represent your added value and set you apart from you competitors. Shared knowledge and lessons learned by those who faced the same problems may not provide the answer but it's an accelerant, an optimization of one's time. You get the advantages of the best practices and experiences of others, allowing you to spend your time on something else. Something more challenging, something more complex, and something more fun.

Reinventing the wheel can become a cover-story for procrastination. We often delude ourselves into thinking that we're being productive by trying to come up with a better way to do something, when we're really just trying to avoid *doing* it. Trying to reinvent the wheel rarely moves you much further down the road. Progress is made by getting in the car and using the wheels that are already on it. Learning to work with what you've got will free up a lot of time and energy that you can use toward actual forward movement. Again, I'm certainly not suggesting that all existing solutions are perfect. There's always a real need for continual improvement. But, if someone's already come up with a solid solution, use it. That will give you more time to tackle problems that have no solutions at all. And that will be true progress.

As you go out into the world today, or lay your head down to go to sleep tonight, remember this: You don't have to reinvent the wheel to be successful, you just have to learn from others mistakes. Study someone who's already done it and figure out what they did. Chances are if you've learned it from someone who's already been successful, it'll work. But you'll never know until you actually try it. Having tried to reinvent the wheel many times myself, I can personally vouch for the fact that it's beneficial to leave well-enough alone. As the saying goes, "*if it ain't broke, don't fix it.*" There's no sense in starting at square one when you can start at square ten.

CHAPTER 8

Stop Talking About It and Start Doing It!

"People may doubt what you say but they will believe what you do."
–Lewis Cass

I have a few pet peeves. One of them is when people know better but choose not to do better. Another one is when people talk about doing something but never do it. As I get older, I run into more and more people that just want to talk about what they want to do, or are going to do, instead of actually doing something about it. They'll talk about the plans they used to have. They'll talk about the goals they are working on now. They'll talk about the life they want to live. And they'll even talk about a few minor obstacles in their way. But in the end, it's just talk. They never take the first step. They never put their talk into action. The way I see it is you only have two choices. You can spend your days dreaming of a better life, or you can get your hands dirty and do the hard work to live out your vision. Let's face it, nobody gets changed by an idea, and nothing gets shaken by a bunch of dreams. Now don't get me wrong, I love dreams and I'm a big fan of ideas. They are the fuel for change in the world. But by themselves, they do absolutely nothing. No actions equal no results.

As I get older, I find myself not wanting to be around people that just talk. I will be incredibly enthusiastic and supportive in any way possible to help you accomplish your goal. But as soon as I realize that you're just talk, I'm out. I tell my little brother and younger cousin all the time, I don't want to hear what you want to do or what you're going to do, I want to see you do it. Actions, as they say, speak louder than words, but words are easier to say and not actually do. If God gave you the vision then go to work. Hanging out in coffee shops and talking about one day being an author, missionary or entrepreneur is the worst thing you can do. Stop telling people about your plans and implement them. Don't dream about being an author, begin writing. Don't talk about being a missionary, go. Don't dream about owning your own business, launch something. Even if it's something small. Successful startups are all about turning ideas into actions. Don't get me wrong, I do recognize that it's these actions that must be the hard part, because both aspiring and seasoned entrepreneurs always seem to come to me with ideas, and ask me for help on the actions. But I can't say it doesn't seem strange to me, since the magic is supposed to be in the ideas, and the actions are about the same for almost every business.

Many businesses spend so much time creating strategies and mission statements but they don't actually implement anything. They plan, analyze, discuss, debate... thinking they are working towards a goal when in fact they are just spinning wheels. Each year, companies spend billions of dollars for education on things such as training, management consultants, seminars, research, books, etc. Management acknowledges that from these activities they are more enlightened or wiser; however, in most cases this knowledge is very seldom actually implemented. As a result, there is very little tangible impact on the organization. The problem in most organizations is not knowing what to do or how to do it – it's just doing it. You've heard the saying, "knowing is half the battle." Well, *doing* is the other half. Having the knowledge to do well in business is important. Having the courage and the ambition to execute what you know, and the momentum and commitment to continue, is what many people lack. Companies need to develop an attitude of action; understanding, planning, and deciding are just the first few steps; actually 'doing' is what counts.

Even if you aren't sure about what you should do, at some point you have to try something. Once you take action, you'll find out what works and what doesn't and if you like it or you don't. See what the results are, adjust your approach, and then try it again. You may find yourself surprised at how you'll find ways to do things faster, cheaper and better and you may even find people who want to join you. But before you can start, you've got to stop talking. You might not get the exact results you were hoping for, but it's not the end of the world. Take note of what you did and what happened, and then do something different next time. If you never take action, you'll never know what is possible and what is not. You will live in misery, as you spend the rest of your life wondering what would have happened if...

Stop talking and start doing. You might be wondering, what's the harm in talking about stuff? When dealing with a problem, people act as if discussing it and preparing plans for action are the same as actually fixing it. If you constantly talk about your ideas and all the things you are going to do yet never deliver, people might start to lose faith in you. People might stop taking you seriously when you start talking about your plan, which can tarnish you on both a professional and personal level. I've been talking about and toying with the idea of being a published author for a long time now. As a child, I started writing poetry and, inspired by Maya Angelou, I often spoke of writing and publishing a collection of my poems as a book. My girlfriend and I have even discussed co-authoring a book together about our experiences and escape from a terribly abusive relationship that we both were involved in, in hopes of being of influence to other young ladies that may be in similar situations. After my mom passed, I started back writing but never completed a book about the life of a ladybug, because I felt like my mother, who we called ladybug, had a story that she never got to tell and so much more to offer to those inspired by her. But now that I've quit talking about it, I've been able to make some progress, and becoming a published author is now being crossed off my bucket list. Whoop there it is, yay me! And that's the way life tends to go, with progress happening only after you shut up and commit yourself to action.

People are always fascinated by successful companies. Many business books have a large dose of what successful companies do, and such information certainly can be helpful. But learning by reading, training programs, and university-based degree programs will get you only so far. Competitive advantage comes from being able to do something others can't do. Anyone can read a book or attend a seminar. The trick is in turning the knowledge acquired into appropriate action. Our tagline at Beyond Visionary Personal & Professional Coaching is "making successful people even MORE successful," with the idea that we only want to work with those who are results-oriented and have true passion and ambition to follow through with their words and plans. Those who won't just talk about it but will be about it and take claim of what's theirs because they understand plans are useless without action. You might like the idea of launching your book, blog or business and all of the attention and interest it generates but there is a lot of blood, sweat and tears in between the starting, finishing and launching.

We often talk about waiting for the perfect timing, the perfect plan, the perfect people or the perfect tools. But life isn't about perfection, it's about progress. And the more action you take the more progress you make. Taking action now is what gets you closer and closer to your dreams. If you are struggling with motivating yourself to take action, practice these next three steps and avoid missing opportunities to successfully achieve your goals.

The first step to taking action is to develop a detailed vision of the future. Visualize your plans being accomplished. See it clearly and vividly. Imagine that you traveled in a time machine into your future and you're filming every aspect of your life... your business... your career. What does the big picture and the details look like three years out? What do you see as the epitome of your success? Don't worry about how you're going to get there; just focus on describing what you see over the next three years. Now, analyze your current lifestyle to determine if you are headed into the wanted direction. Too many times we allow life to happen without us being in the driver's seat. Usually this leads to a lot of what-ifs when looking back on missed opportunities. If you are not satisfied with your current path in life, change the scenery and reroute the destination. You only have one life, so live it by realizing your dreams and accomplishing those things that currently seem impossible.

The second step to successfully achieve your goals is to plan and prepare for the future. Success does not just suddenly occur one day in someone's life; it is a strategic choice that requires due diligence and patience. And those who live successful lives have to keep making that choice every day through planning and preparation. You must do the same. By failing to plan, you are planning to fail. We are all eager for our moment in glory when the hard work finally pays off but until that time comes, continue moving forward. Keep yourself motivated by keeping your eye on the prize and using that image as unlimited fuel to remain focused.

The final step to take action fulfill your dreams is to execute your plan. Nothing can be accomplished without executing a game plan. No matter how brilliant the person or how revolutionary the idea, that means nothing if the idea has no action behind it. Do not settle on your ideas being the selling point because millions of people have ideas, but only a few can make their ideas a reality. If you want to make it happen badly enough; you will strive relentlessly to make your ideas and concepts known to the public. Put your ideas into motion and generate interest through a well-executed game plan that illustrates your hunger to be taken seriously.

It's no secret; life is what you make it. It is only when you stop talking about what you want to do and take action, will you begin to see your vision unfold. Your life will grow. Your business will expand. Your health will improve. Your finances will multiply. Your family will prosper. And your actions will speak louder than your words. Because taking action is the only way to change your circumstances and possibly the world around you. Remember it's never too late to be what you might have been, and it's never too late to take action.

About the Author

Like you, Personal and Professional Development Expert Kelli Rogers aspires to live a life of significance and purpose, full of great relationships, excitement and personal success. But what are the secrets to a fulfilling life? Is love and happiness really all that matter? Or is it more about money and power? How do you know that you have achieved success?

With over a decade of business, life and career coaching, speaking, and most importantly, real life, in-the-trenches business experience, Kelli is committed to showing people how to achieve better results in their personal and professional lives. Unlike many coaches, she is not in business to make her as much money as possible; it's about creating opportunities for YOU to make as much money as possible. Kelli appreciates, and shares with her audience, that "I'm only successful, if you're successful," while working her a$$ off to ensure her clients are happy and receive quick, convenient results. No reasons... Just results! Because "anyone can have anything, if you're willing to do the work."

Kelli is the founder and CEO of Beyond Visionary Personal & Professional Coaching. She is a Professional Certified Coach and a Licensed Masters Social Worker. Kelli has partnered with both aspiring and seasoned entrepreneurs and small business leaders to develop and implement beneficial strategies to take them to the next level. She continues to coach the best and the brightest individuals to identify their strengths, set SMART goals and achieve a higher level of prosperity in their personal and professional development. Kelli also delights in partnering with groups and organizations that strive to not only make a difference in their own lives, but the lives of others and the world at large.

As a successful entrepreneur, Kelli's primary mission is to empower people to be courageous and attain their goals and desires, while creating a renewed sense of passion and purpose. Her presentation style has been known to stir up a group, while her coaching skills bring out the best in people. For several years, Kelli has supported her clients through life and business transitions and the achievement of their dreams utilizing various innovative coaching systems and techniques, including both a strength-based perspective and solution-focused approach.

For booking and inquiries please contact: kelli.rogers@beyondvisionary.net

www.ingramcontent.com/pod-product-compliance
Lightning Source LLC
Chambersburg PA
CBHW071122210326
41519CB00020B/6384